李山山水画集

LANDSCAPE PAINTINGS BY LI SHAN

淑馨出版社

（封面畫） 今日陽光燦爛

（Cover）　Brilliant Sunshine today

畫家 李 山
LI SHAN

李山——藝術簡歷

1926 年	生於中國山東省青島海濱。
1948 年	畢業於四川國立六中。
1958 年	畢業於浙江美術學院。
	新疆畫報社畫家。
1960 年	作品參加 1960 年全國美展。
1961 年	畫《天山月初升》陳列於人民大會堂・北京
1962 年	江蘇省國畫院畫家。
	作品參加 1962 年全國美展。
1963 年	作品參加 1963 年全國美展。
1965 年	爲中國美術家協會會員。
1973 年	作品在香港集古齋《中國近代名家書畫展覽》展出。
1978 年	作品在香港博雅藝術公司《中國名家書畫展覽》展出。
1980 年	被選爲南京美術協會副主席。
	受聘爲巢湖國畫院名譽院長。
	作品在日本東京《中國榮寶齋展覽》展出。
	《李山中國畫展》在南京博物院展出。
	電視台在全國播出《畫中詩——介紹李山的中國畫》。
1981 年	在美國定居。
	《李山畫展》在美國紐約三友齋舉行。
	《李山畫展》在美國林肯市蕭爾頓美術館舉行。
	《李山畫展》在尼布拉斯加州立大學奧馬哈分校舉行，美國。
	《李山花鳥畫展》在美國舊金山中華文化中心舉行。
	《李山畫展》在美國卡麥爾市古物畫廊舉行。
	講學於美國尼布拉斯加州立大學，聖陶瑪斯大學，休斯敦婦女學院，米德蘭學院，海斯汀學院，貝爾威學院，康考地亞教師學院，威斯廉大學，道奈學院，汝尼學院。
	《李山》畫册在紐約三友齋出版。
	《中國美術家人名辭典》介紹李山，上海人民美術出版社出版。
1982 年	《中國藝術家辭典》現代第三分册介紹李山，湖南出版社出版。
	《李山新疆畫集》出版。
	《李山畫展》在新加坡海鷗畫廊舉行。
	《李山畫展》在美國佩支畫廊舉行。

1983 年　《李山畫展》在美國綠蔭道畫廊舉行。
　　　　《李山畫展》在馬來西亞·吉隆坡·集珍莊畫廊舉行。
　　　　爲美國威斯廉大學客座教授。
　　　　列入《當代中國畫》英文版推薦的 90 位畫家之一。
　　　　《中國現代書畫篆刻家名鑒》介紹李山·日本·東京。
1985 年　《李山書畫展》在新加坡海鷗畫廊舉行。
1986 年　《李山畫選》出版。
　　　　《李山畫展》在美國德克薩州立大學達拉斯分校舉行。
1988 年　《李山畫展》在美國普蘭黛穆畫廊舉行。
1989 年　《李山畫展》在台北雄獅畫廊舉行。
1990 年　《李山·葛新民二人展》在日本名古屋舉行。
1991 年　《李山畫展》在美國紐約聖約翰大學亞洲中心畫廊舉行。
1992 年　再去中國新疆天山牧區寫生。

作品被收藏於：
　　　　中國美術館。
　　　　人民大會堂·北京。
　　　　南京博物院。
　　　　吉林博物館。
　　　　杜甫草堂。
　　　　浙江美術學院。
　　　　新加坡南洋美專。
　　　　美國蕭爾頓美術館。

LI SHAN—A Biographical Sketch

1926–	Born in Qintao, China
1953–1958	Studied at the Zhejiang Art Institute.
1958–1966	Editor of the Xingjiang Art Pictorial
	Artist in Jiangsu Chinese Painting Insttitue
1980–	Honorary Presiddent of the Chao-Hu Chinese painting Institute
	Vice-president of the Nanjing Artist Association
	Nanjing Museum one-man exhibition
	Television documentary program aired nationwide by China Centrel
	Broadcasting Bureau, entitled "The Chinese Paintings of LiShan"
1981–1990	visit to the U. S. A.
	One-man exhibition at
	Three Friends Studio Gallery/New York
	Sheldon Gallery/Lincoln, Nebraska
	Gallery Antique/Camel, California
	Paige Gallery/Dallas, Texas
	Boulevard Gallery/Huston, Texas
	University of Texas at Dallas
	Plandome Gallery/Long Island, NY.
	Sea-Gull Gallery/Singapore
	The Art House/Kuala Lumpur, Malaysia
	Lion Gallery/Taipei, R.O.C.
	Visiting professor of the Texas Wesleyan College,Fort worth, Texas
1991–	One-man exhibition at St. John's University. New York.

Professional publications featuring Li's work

Li Shan's Xingniang Paintings by the Xingjiang People's Publishing Co. China

Li Shan's Paintings by the Jiangsu People's Publication Co. China

Who's Who of Chinese Art, by the Shanghai people's Art Publishing Co. China.

Who's Who of Contemporary Chinese Art, Vol.3, by the Hunan People's Publishing Co. China

Chinese Painters and Calligraphists, published by Chinese Gallery, Japan.

Contemporary Chinese Painting by the New World Press, China

Major Museums and Public Offices which own Mr.Li's. work as part of their permanent collection
Great Hall of the People, Tian an Men Square,Peking.
The National Fine Art Museum, Peking.
Jilin Museum, China
Nanjing Museum, China
Zhejiang Art Institute, China
Sheldon Gallery, Lincoln, Nebraska. U. S. A.

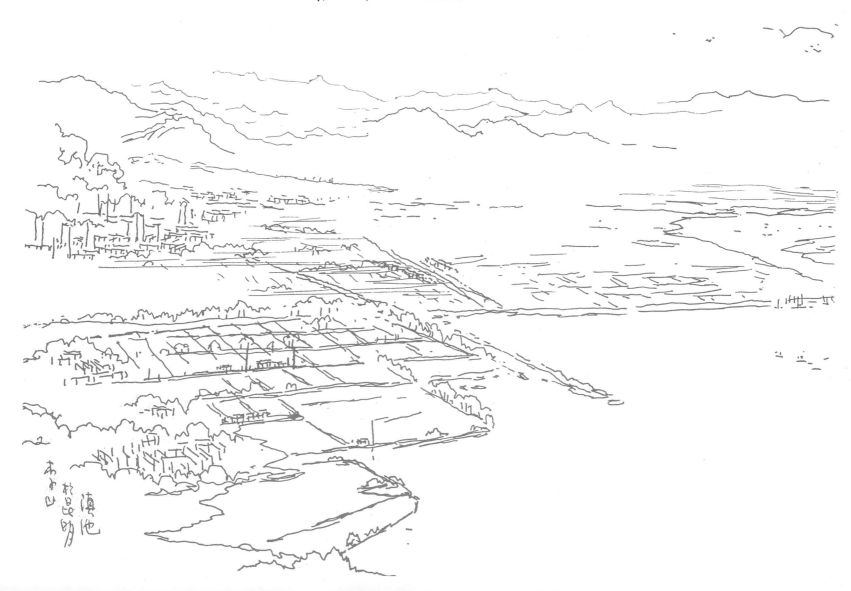

讀山水詩筆記

· 李山 ·

山水詩，其實也就是一幅山水畫。

詩與畫，在表達手段上當然並不相同，但決定一件藝術作品的高低，最終在於通過藝術手段所達成的最後效果——感人心靈的境界。這在詩與畫都是一致的。研究優秀的詩篇在境界上所達到的深度，這對繪畫創作是很有裨益的。

杜甫，這位偉大的詩人，《春望》一詩，僅只其中的四句，便足以震動千古。「國破山河在，城春草木深，感時花濺淚，恨別鳥驚心。」至今我們讀來，猶能感受到唐代安史之亂時那戰火離亂，生民塗炭的悲慘景象，使我們看到了一個歷史時代。

「鬱孤台下清江水，中間多少行人淚，西北望長安，可憐無數山。」（宋·辛棄疾），黯然的羣山，悲泣的江水，重山之外，更遠處是被金兵侵占了的北方山河。作品在悲涼的景色中，表達出了對家國命運之深情。

「亂石崩雲，驚濤裂岸，捲起千堆雪。江山如畫，一時多少豪傑。」（宋·蘇東坡）激浪驚濤，當其撞擊飛濺時，瑰麗如紛崩之雲，如千推之雪。詩寫的是江濤景色，其實表達的是作者對三國時一代眾多英雄豪傑的燦爛業績之讚揚。讀者也自然會隨之被鼓舞起向上之豪情。

元曲，王實甫《西廂記》長亭送別一折寫離別之景色：「碧雲天，黃花地，西風緊，北雁南飛。曉來誰染霜林醉，總是離人淚。」深秋，遠處那經霜後的樹林，是誰把它染成了一片如醉了的紅色呢？啊，那都是離人在哭泣時哭出血的眼淚所染成的啊。這一段風景詩句，已成了對人間至性至情最深刻的表達。

「離離原上草，一歲一枯榮，野火燒不盡，春風吹又生。」（唐·白居易）景色是原野上一大片被燒焦了的草地，卻在黝黑的焦草中，又生出了小小嫩綠的草芽。這種景色所流露的倔強精神將給讀者在意志上以多大的鼓舞！這實在是太高明的藝術創作。

在古詩中，有很多對落日景色的描寫，但境界各不相同。

「大漠孤煙直，長河落日圓。」（唐·王維）境界雄渾壯麗，讀之使人心胸開闊。

「荒城臨古渡，落日滿秋山」（唐·王維）滿山上，每一片秋葉都抹上了夕陽的光輝，金光閃爍，使人衷心地讚嘆這大自然的美麗。

「青山依舊在，幾度夕陽紅。」（元·羅貫中）人世滄桑幾經變幻，但青山無恙，屹立至今。意境傷感，但使人曠達。

這些古代優秀詩人的作品對於我的繪畫創作曾給以極大的啟示。在我畫三峽的激浪時，我賦予這激浪以勇士般博鬥的精神；在我畫大海時，我希望畫出生命永遠奔騰不息的歌聲；當我畫晚秋的樹林時，我希望畫出雖然已在酷霜之後，但卻依然歡笑樂觀的情懷；當我畫到故國雄峙的山嶺時，我希望表達出那銅牆鐵壁般的氣概，卻又有涼涼泉水的柔情，為了這樣的山河，才使我們世世代代多少英雄兒女為之付出了自己的生命。

深沉的意境，畢竟是詩的靈魂，也是畫的靈魂。

Notes Taken While Reading Landscape Poetry

Li Shan

Landscape poems in a sense are landscape paintings. Although they are totally different in their particular means of representation, the yardstick I use to measure the depth to which either has achieved the fullest artistic expression–is the same. If the work touches the heart, if the final effect is deeply felt, then the poet or painter has achieved the highest virtue.

I study the great poets and search for that emotional depth. I read again the words of Tu–Fu,and I am deeply moved.

The country is on the verge of collapse,

But hills and rivers remain.

In spring the grass and leaves grow thick in the city.

The flowers shed tears for the troubled times.

And the birds seem startled as if with the anguish of separation.

In one stanza the great poet Tu–Fu carries me back in time to the Tang Dynasty. I can still feel the suffering of the people during the An–Lu–Shan Revolt. I view through his words that miserable period in history; these words echo through thousands of years.

And with these words by the poet Xin Qi–Ji of the Sung Dynasty, I paint a sorrowful picture in my mind's eye.

In the river below Gloomy Terrace, I wonder

How many tears shed by refugees

Were immersed in its clean water.

Looking north-west toward Chang–An,

I see but numberless gloomy mountains.

I see the gloomy hills and weeping river, and far away in the north, there are more mountains and rivers occupied by the invading enemy. In depicting this melancholy scene, the poet expressed his deep concern for the fate of his country, for my native country. I glimpse the soul of the poet and try to seize it with my brush.

And again I draw inspiration from this poem by Su Tun–Po of the Sung Dynasty.

The tumbling rocks thrust into the air,

The roaring surges dash upon the shore,

Rolling into a thousand drifts of snow.

The river and the mountains make a vivid picture—

What a host of heros once were

The roaring waters, while splashing and crashing upon the shore, look like a thousand drifts of snow. On the surface, this was a description of a scene of river surges. Nevertheless, it actually expressed the poet's admiration and praise for the heroes and their brilliant deeds during the Three–Kingdom period.

In The Story of the West Wing, (Which was written in the form of "qu", a poetic style especially popular in the Yuan Dynasty), the author, Wang Shih–Fu, wrote the following sentences to describe the scene of departure, as two lovers bid farewell at the Tall pavilion.

Under the blue cloudy sky,

Yellow flowers flourish in the field.

The west wind blows fast,

And the wild geese in the north are flying to the south.

Who has reddened the frost–covered forest at dawn as if it were drunk

Oh, who else except the departing lovers in full tears.

In this description of landscape, Wang Shih–Fu expresses the anguish of the departing lovers, their tears bathing the frost–covered forest red. The poet speaks of the most ardent, romantic love, the strongest passion in human lives so poignantly.

And I am inspired by Pai Chu–Yi's poem, (from the Tang Dynasty.) I see his use of nature as a metaphor for the renaissance of the human spirit.

How luxuriant the grass in the meadow,

Flourishing and decaying in a single year!

Even fire will not burn it up,

For the spring breeze will blow it to life again.

I visualize the meadow on which a large part of the grass has been scorched, and yet small shoots of soft grass are growing from the blackened roots again. What a firm and perseverant spirit this word picture reveals! It is a great inspiration to my creative work that I gain from these ancient, excellent poems.

When I create the painting of the surging waves in the Three Gorges, I entrust the struggling spirit of the warrior to the surging waves. When I paint the picture of the ocean, I hope the song of the incessantly rolling pattern of life is expressed.

When I bring forth the painting of Late Autumn Forest, I hope the hearty laughter, the optimistic feeling is expressed, even if it happens after the bitter frost.

When I create the painting of the magnificent mountains of my native country, I hope to express its spirit as a bastion of iron and the tenderness of the murmuring spring; in these mountains, many fine sons and daughters of our country have given their lives, from generation to generation, to this beautiful mother land.

After all, the depth of feeling is the soul of the peom and that of the painting as well.

Translated by Shu–Liang Lo

目 錄 Contents

1 山雨欲來

Moments before a rainfall in the mountain

69cm×68cm

2　潮水升
Tide rising
46cm×69cm

3　雨打風吹三月暮

A storm in late March

68cm×69cm

4 野渡
A ferry in the countryside
68cm×68cm

5 雪溶
Snow melting
69cm×46cm

6 搏鬥的三峽
The struggling Three Gorges
45cm×67cm

7　雪
Snow
33cm×45cm

8　春已至，殘雪猶自戀湖山
Spring now, snow still remaining on lakes and mountains
44cm×66cm

9 趁得風雪稍息間，滿山開遍紅杜鵑

In the suspension of a snow storm, red azaleas grow all
over the mountain

69cm×69cm

10 浪花，奔騰的浪花
Waves, storming waves
43cm×66cm

11 春去也，天上人間

Spring is gone. In heaven or on earth?

45cm×60cm

12　這歡笑的秋天
This hilarious autumn
45cm×69cm

13 觀滄海
Looking out to sea
34cm×138cm

14　細雨已過猶含烟

After drizzle it is still misty over the mountain

69cm×68cm

15 憶寫神州好山河

Beautiful scenery of mainland China in my memory

70cm×136cm

16 相看兩不厭，只有敬亭山
Ging-Tin, the only mountain
that I will never be tired of
looking at and that will never be tired of me either.
46cm×57cm

17 風飄大荒寒
Cold wind blowing over the
field
70cm×46cm

18　夏雨
Summer rain
106cm×35cm

19 聽濤
Listening to the waves
65cm×67cm

20　峯廻路轉處，又過一重山
Turning to the other side, there is another ridge
69cm×46cm

21　暮靄萬重山

Mountains beyond mountains in the sunset glow

60cm×67cm

22　山水壯行去萬里，猶聞絮絮惜別聲
On a sightseeing trip thousands of miles sway, farewell
greetings still click in the ear.
45cm×69cm

23 海上升明月
The moon rising from the sea
70cm×70cm

24　山中一夜雨，樹梢百重泉
An overnight rainfall in the
mountain creates hundreds
of little springs from the
tops of trees
96cm×59cm

25 江河不擇細流
Rivers never reject streams and brooks
84cm×47cm

26　江南明月夜
A moonlit night in the south
region of the Yangtze
Valley
69cm×69cm

27　料知白雲下，尚有山泉飛
Anticipated that there will be flying mountain streams
under the white cloud.
34cm×69cm

28　晨霧
Morning fog
77cm×68cm

29　天山

Tien-Shan Mountain

67cm×132cm

30　晨霧漸消見天山
Tien-Shan Mountain appears as the
morning fog gradually disperses.

47cm×101cm

31 太平天國石船

Stone boat of the Taiping Kingdom

43cm×64cm

32 南京瞻園

Zhan Garden in Nanking

43cm×63cm

33　聽濤

Listening to waves

45cm×69cm

34　薄暮月凌波

The moonlight reflecting on waves in the evening

46cm×69cm

35　樹老又有新枝出，敢與雪山爭短長

New branches growing up from the old trunk, dare compete with the snow mountain for attention.

51cm×70cm

36 迷花倚石忽已暝

Leaning on the rock, fascinated by flowers, unaware that it is already dusk.

69cm×45cm

37　白雲飄紗戀青山

White cloud lingering on the green
mountain as if in love with it

46cm×69cm

38　山林初醒
The hill and the forest just woke up
69cm×139cm

39　只在此山中，雲深不知處

Only aware of being in this mountain, but not of exact
whereabouts because of the deep cloud

68cm×69cm

40 悲號的山河
The crying mountains and rivers
68cm×68cm

41 驟雨初歇

A sudden rain just let up

69cm×92cm

42 平沙落雁

A flock of wild geese swoops
on the flat sands

49cm×90cm

43　霧失烟波路

The smoky track of waves faded into the fog

70cm×70cm

44 秋風涼
The autumn wind is cool
69cm×59cm

45　太湖秋

Tai-Hu Lake in autumn

46cm×69cm

46 旭日照天山
Sunshine over Tien-Shan Mountain
40cm×67cm

47 聽峽谷日夜走江濤

The torrent through the gorge can be heard day and
night.

46cm×69cm

48　流泉每依山花畔，日日夜夜訴衷情
Waterfalls always lean on the bank of wild flowers in order to express their love for them day and night.
69cm×68cm

49 水鄉
Waterscape
34cm×45cm

50 明月自徘徊
The moon is lingering above the trees
70cm×103cm

51　含笑山花次第來

Smiling mountain flowers blossom successively

69cm×68cm

52 登高
Mountain climbing
66cm×43cm

53　賽里木湖
Lake Salimu
68cm×137cm

54　春雪
Spring snow
70cm×52cm

55　秋色天山路

A Tien-Shan Mountain path in autumn

101cm×83cm

56　聽江濤
Listening to the river surges
44cm×66cm

57　牧童歌
A buffalo boy's song
65cm×43cm

58 臨波
By the waterside
64cm×88cm

59　泉韻

The rhythm of the waterfall

58cm×47cm

60　但願人長久，千里共嬋娟
Wishing we all live long ang share the same moonlight
even separated a thousand miles away
69cm×70cm

61 走天山

Riding on horseback to Tien-Shan Mountain

83cm×68cm

62 聽流泉
Listening to the waterfall
66cm×65cm

63 不知天上宮闕今夕是何年
What is the year in the
Heavenly Palace of this
time? I wonder.
69cm×45cm

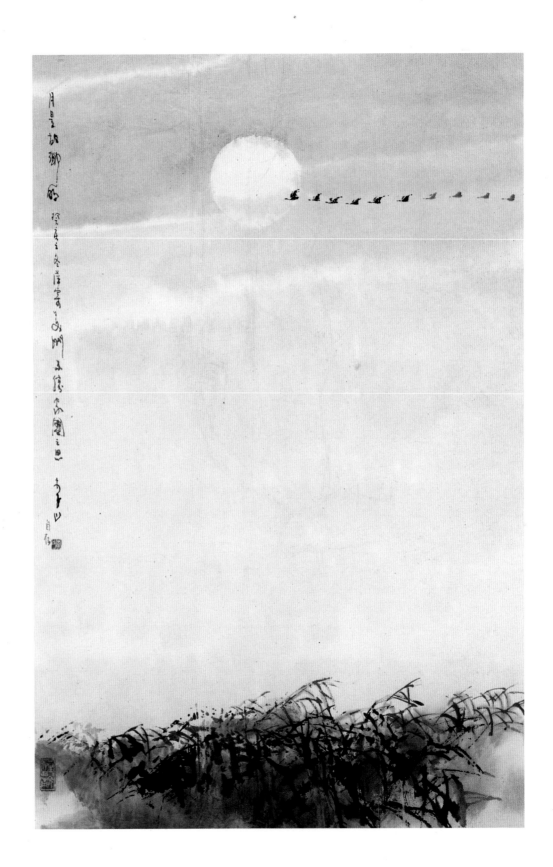

64 月是故鄉明

The moonlight in one's native land is brighter than
anywhere else

67cm×45cm

出 版 後 記

　　我們在相繼出版了《李山畫集》、《李山花鳥畫集》之後，再出版了《李山山水畫集》。

　　這本畫集的特色在於作品中濃郁的詩情。它牽動著讀者的心，遠走出了畫面之外，使人感受到家國的動盪、人生的拼博，和山河雲霞的歡笑與嘆息。讀者當也會感覺到中國古典文化的精華在這些作品中的延續。

　　在出版者的使命而言，豐實讀者的文化世界，拓展中華文化的精華，這也正是我們的重要目標，因此，我們樂於看到本册的發行。

淑馨出版社發行人

陸又雄　謹誌

The Publisher's Remarks

After we successively published <u>Paintings By Li–Shan</u> and <u>The Flower–Bird Paintings By Li–Shan</u>, we have now published <u>The Landscape Paintings By Li–Shan.</u>

The feature of this book is its deep poetic taste that permeates all the paintings. It attracts the reader's (viewers') hearts far behond the picture to a more complecated scene. It makes them feel the turmoil of our country, the struggle of life, the happy laughter and sad groans of the mountains and rivers as well as clouds. The readers (viewers) will also feel that the most exquisite Chinese classic continues among these artistic works.

So far as my mission as the publisher is concerned, to enrich the reader's culture world and to develop the ethos of Chinese culture is precisely our primary goal. Therefore, we have great pleasure in seeing this painting book published.

Yu–Hung Luk
Publisher
Shu Shin Publishing Co.

國立中央圖書館出版品預行編目資料

李山山水畫集=Landscape paintings by Li
Shan/李山著. --初版. --臺北市：淑馨
，民83
面；　公分
ISBN 957-531-374-7(平裝)

1.繪畫-中國-作品集　2.山水畫-作品集

945.6　　　　　　　　　　　　　83005896

李山　山水畫集
LANDSCAPE PAINTINGS BY LI SHAN

著　　　者／李山	Author／Li Shan
發 行 人／陸又雄	Publisher／Luk Yuhung
翻　　　譯／羅叔艮	Translation／Lo Shuliang
攝　　　影／張冠豪	Photograph／Chang Kuanhao
責任編輯／尤淑芬	Editor／You Shwufen
出 版 者／淑馨出版社	Published by／Shushin Books
地　　　址／台北市安和路二段65號2樓	Address／2F, No. 65, Anho Road, Sec. 2, Taipei, Taiwan
電　　　話／7039867・7006285	Telephone／886-7039867・7006285
傳　　　眞／7084804	Fax／886-2-7084804
郵　　　撥／0534577～5 淑馨出版社	Printed by／Shine Color Printing CO., LTD.
印　　　刷／六景彩印實業有限公司	Law Adviser／Xiunglin Xian
法律顧問／蕭雄淋律師	First Edition／August 1994
登 記 證／新聞局局版台業字第2613號	Price／USD 20.00
版　　　次／1994年（民國83年）8月初版	Copyright by Shushin Books
定　　　價／400元	All Rights reserved